T0082424

Sun and Moon

THIS EDITION
Editorial Management by Oriel Square
Produced for DK by WonderLab Group LLC
Jennifer Emmett, Erica Green, Kate Hale, *Founders*

Editors Grace Hill Smith, Libby Romero, Michaela Weglinski;
Photography Editors Kelley Miller, Annette Kiesow, Nicole DiMella;
Managing Editor Rachel Houghton; **Designers** Project Design Company;
Researcher Michelle Harris; **Copy Editor** Lori Merritt; **Indexer** Connie Binder;
Proofreader Larry Shea; **Reading Specialist** Dr. Jennifer Albro; **Curriculum Specialist** Elaine Larson

Published in the United States by DK Publishing
1745 Broadway, 20th Floor, New York, NY 10019

Copyright © 2023 Dorling Kindersley Limited
DK, a Division of Penguin Random House LLC
22 23 24 25 26 10 9 8 7 6 5 4 3 2 1
001-333849-May/2023

A catalog record for this book
is available from the Library of Congress.
HC ISBN: 978-0-7440-7091-0
PB ISBN: 978-0-7440-7092-7

DK books are available at special discounts when purchased in bulk for sales promotions, premiums,
fundraising, or educational use. For details, contact: DK Publishing Special Markets,
1745 Broadway, 20th Floor, New York, NY 10019
SpecialSales@dk.com

Printed and bound in China

The publisher would like to thank the following for their kind permission to reproduce their images:
a=above; c=center; b=below; l=left; r=right; t=top; b/g=background

Dorling Kindersley: NASA 8br; **Dreamstime.com:** Awargula 30cr, Fokusgood 6-7, Andrey Kotko / Raccoonn 11bl, Brian
Kushner / Bkushner 22clb, Matthieuclouis 7c, Paulpaladin 8-9, Procyab 7bl, Chiew Ropram 24-25b, Jekaterina Sahmanova
9br, Smileus 10br, Nuttawut Uttamaharad 5tr; **Getty Images:** DigitalVision / Ariel Skelley 20br, Stone / Hans Neleman 5c;
NASA: 28-29; **Shutterstock.com:** 19 STUDIO 23, Mihai_Andritoiu 20-21, Artsiom P 27cb, AstroStar 26-27, buradaki 6br,
CandyRetriever 21bl, Castleski 28br, 29b, 31bl, herle_catharina 31cl, Mee Ko Dong 4crb, 12-13, 30crb, Elena11 27bl,
EpicStockMedia 30, Juergen Faelchle 17cb, Graphics999 15b, LedyX 31tl, mapichai 19b, Nostalgia for Infinity 3clb, 26br,
31clb, Onkamon 3crb, 8cl, 30cra, otsphoto 11br, Photoartdesign 16br, Anuruk Pongpatimet 30br, Redsapphire 24-25,
Ricardo Reitmeyer 16-17, 31cla, SedmogJula10 13c, Aleksandra Suzi 5br, Johan Swanepoel 18-19, titoOnz 10-11, 14-15, TNK
DESIGN 13bl, Peter Togel 9bl, Vibrant Image Studio 14br, Kayla Wolfe 4cr, XiXinXing 12br

Cover images: *Front:* **Dreamstime.com:** Valerii Brozhinskii, Yusuf Demirci br, Koryaba cra, Zeechinchun cl;
Shutterstock.com: Nostalgia for Infinity tr

All other images © Dorling Kindersley
For more information see: www.dkimages.com

For the curious
www.dk.com

Sun and Moon

Libby Romero

The Sun and the Moon are important to Earth. Let us learn why!

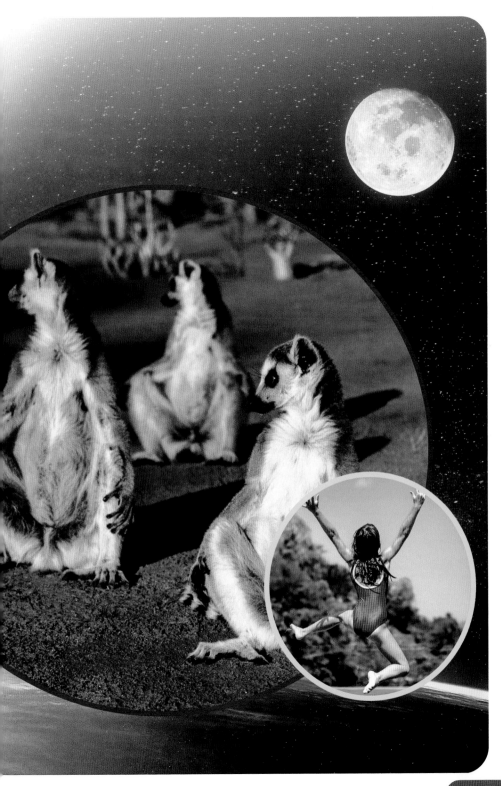

The Sun is a star.
The Sun is a hot ball
of gas.

star

Sun

A moon is a dusty ball of rock.
Earth has one Moon.

Moon

moon

Earth

The Sun makes energy.

The Sun's energy
goes to Earth
as light and heat.

Sun's light

energy
[EH-ner-jee]

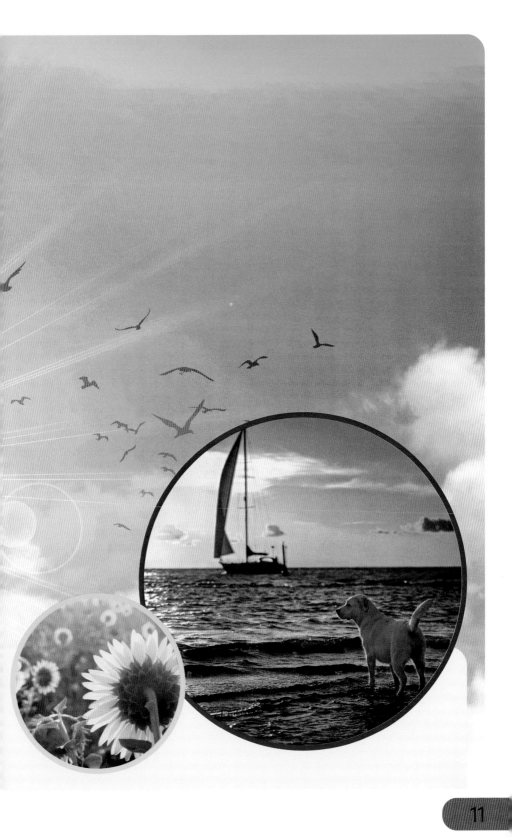

Plants and animals need light and heat to live.

live

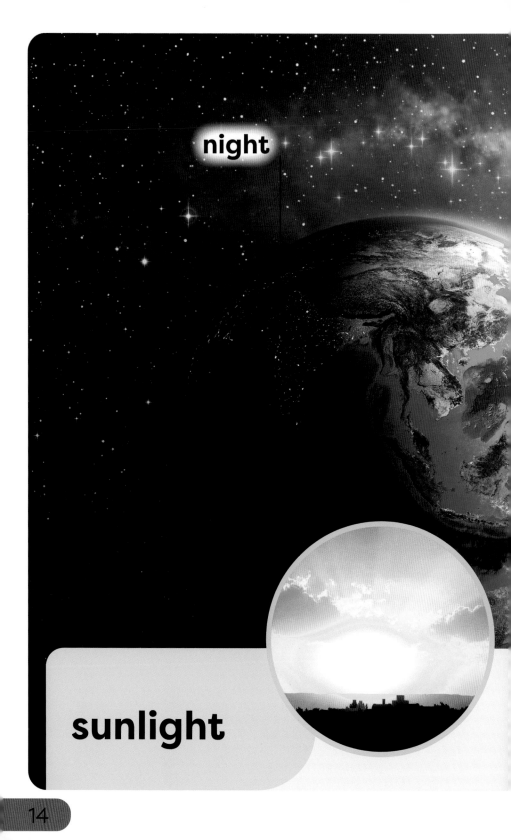

night

sunlight

Sunlight shines
on one side of Earth.
Earth turns.
Sunlight shines
on the other side.
That is why Earth
has day and night.

day

Sunlight shines
on the Moon.
Light bounces off
the Moon.
That is why the
Moon glows.

moon glow

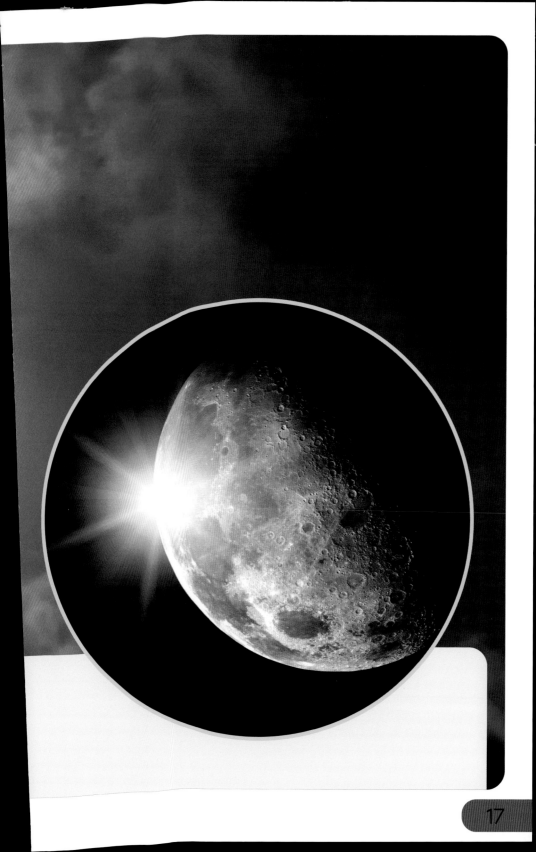

Earth travels around the Sun.

Earth

travel

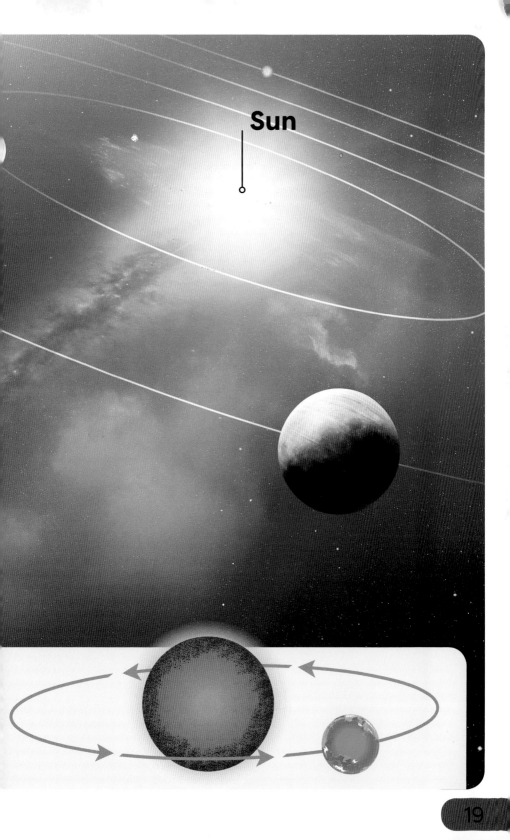

Sun

Earth is tilted.
The side leaning
toward the Sun
is hotter.
That is why Earth
has seasons.

seasons

The Moon moves
around Earth.
As it moves,
our view of
the Moon changes.

view of the moon

gibbous moon

Earth

full moon

moon's shape

That is why the Moon looks like it changes shape.

new moon

crescent moon

People study the Sun and the Moon.
They use spacecraft.
They use telescopes.

spacecraft
[SPAYS-kraft]

telescope

spacecraft

Astronauts have even gone to the Moon!

astronaut

[A-struh-NAAT]

Earth would not be the same without the Sun and the Moon.

Glossary

astronaut
a person trained to work and travel in outer space

energy
natural power;
the ability to make something active

glow
a steady light

seasons
the four parts of the year: spring, summer, fall, and winter

spacecraft
a vehicle designed to travel in outer space

Quiz

Answer the questions to see what you have learned. Check your answers with an adult.

1. What does the Sun give to the Earth?

2. Why does the Moon glow?

3. Why does the Moon look like it changes shape?

4. What are two things people use to study the Sun and the Moon?

5. What do you think astronauts can learn by going to the Moon?

1. Light and heat 2. Sunlight bounces off the moon
3. Our view of the moon changes as it goes around Earth
4. Spacecraft and telescopes 5. Answers will vary